SELECTED CAUT

Hilaire Belloc's classic collec lished nearly fifty years a laughed at and learnt from by children today. The character of Matilda (who told lies) is as naughty and disastrous as ever, and although we laugh, who will ever slam a door again, when they have read what happened to Rebecca?

Cautionary Tales, *Beasts for Bad Children* and two chapters on rather outrageous adults (Peers and Ladies and Gentlemen) make up this witty and much-loved collection.

The verses are accompanied by the original illustrations, which add to the sense of fun, and together they have made *Cautionary Verses* a childhood classic.

Hilaire Belloc was born in France in 1870 and was brought up in France and England. He was a scholar of Balliol College, Oxford, and wrote a great many books before he died in 1953.

H. BELLOC

SELECTED CAUTIONARY VERSES

Revised Puffin Edition
with the original pictures by
B. T. B.
and Nicolas Bentley

PUFFIN BOOKS

Puffin Books, Penguin Books Ltd, Harmondsworth, Middlesex, England
Viking Penguin Inc., 40 West 23rd Street, New York, New York 10010, U.S.A.
Penguin Books Australia Ltd, Ringwood, Victoria, Australia
Penguin Books Canada Limited, 2801 John Street, Markham, Ontario, Canada L3R 1B4
Penguin Books (N.Z.) Ltd, 182–190 Wairau Road, Auckland 10, New Zealand

—

Illustrated album edition first published 1940
Published in Puffin Story Books 1950
Reissued in Penguin Books 1958
Revised Puffin Edition 1964
Reprinted 1966, 1968, 1971, 1972, 1973, 1974, 1975,
1976, 1978, 1979, 1981, 1983, 1987

—

—

Printed and bound in Great Britain by
Cox & Wyman Ltd, Reading
Set in Monotype Perpetua

Cautionary Verses
is the complete album edition of Mr Belloc's humorous verse
from which the selection in this Puffin Book has been
made. In its 407 pages are all the 381 original pictures by
B. T. B. and Nicolas Bentley and all these seven famous books,
unabridged: *Cautionary Tales for Children, More Cautionary Tales,
The Bad Child's Book of Beasts, More Beasts for Worse Children,
A Moral Alphabet, More Peers*, and *Ladies and Gentlemen*.

Child! do not throw this book about;
    Refrain from the unholy pleasure
Of cutting all the pictures out!
    Preserve it as your chiefest treasure.

Child, have you never heard it said
    That you are heir to all the ages?
Why, then, your hands were never made
    To tear these beautiful thick pages!

Your little hands were made to take
    The better things and leave the worse ones.
They also may be used to shake
    The Massive Paws of Elder Persons.

And when your prayers complete the day,
    Darling, your little tiny hands
Were also made, I think, to pray
    For men that lose their fairylands.

CONTENTS

CONTENTS

About Hilaire Belloc

Hilaire Belloc was born in France in 1870, and was brought up in France and England. He was a scholar of Balliol College, Oxford, and wrote a great many books before he died in 1953; but he was always a poor man. Although French and Irish blood ran in his veins he was also an Englishman in every sense of the word.

Belloc was a stimulating companion, never at a loss for conversation or entertainment, and a wit with a true sense of fun and of the ridiculous. This was demonstrated when he went to a lunch of the newly-formed Drakenberg Society, and made a rousing speech about a Danish sailor of whom he had never heard before. This was typical!

I shall never forget him. He taught us much about wine and song, for Belloc broke into song whenever and wherever he felt like it, and drinking wine with his friends was one of his delights. He had a passion for telephoning, but never had a telephone in his own house. Often he arrived at my house saying, 'Can I telephone?', and would then closet himself away for half an hour or more to make his calls.

How can his kaleidoscopic character be described? Religion was the driving force in his life, and the source of his fortitude, strength of mind, and gaiety. He was an unfailing and delightful friend, but he was also obstreperous and intolerant. He had no patience with stupidity, inefficient waiters, bad food, and English politicians. He could be ruder and more courteous, kinder and yet more pugnacious, than any man I have ever met. Sometimes one saw him simply as a pernickety man who fussed about railway timetables or broken tea-cups, but all at once one found oneself in the presence of a Titan inspired with immense knowledge.

He enjoyed the company of children and understood their tastes, particularly their liking for disasters and catastrophes of all kinds, yet the outrageous exaggeration of the calamities that mowed down his characters avoided the sadness or horror of the Little Mermaid and the horrors of Struwwelpeter. His *Cautionary Tales* are true classics; they are unsurpassable. Read 'Jim' and 'Henry King' and you will understand why. Belloc also provides some useful observations on animal behaviour, and a handy guide to the peerage. This collection gives some idea of this remarkable author, and will undoubtedly make readers want to explore further.

H. S. MACKINTOSH

Cautionary Tales
for Children

ILLUSTRATED BY

B. T. B.

Introduction

Upon being asked by a Reader whether the verses contained in this book were true.

And is it True? It is not True.
And if it were it wouldn't do,
For people such as me and you
Who pretty nearly all day long
Are doing something rather wrong.
Because if things were really so,
You would have perished long ago,
And I would not have lived to write
The noble lines that meet your sight,
Nor B. T. B. survived to draw
The nicest things you ever saw.

H. B.

Jim

There was a Boy whose name was Jim;
His Friends were very good to him.
They gave him Tea, and Cakes, and Jam,
And slices of delicious Ham,
And Chocolate with pink inside,
And little Tricycles to ride,
And

———

read him Stories through and through,
And even took him to the Zoo –
But there it was the dreadful Fate
Befell him, which I now relate.

You know – at least you *ought* to know,
For I have often told you so –
That Children never are allowed
To leave their Nurses in a Crowd;

Now this was Jim's especial Foible,
He ran away when he was able,
And on this inauspicious day
He slipped his hand and ran away!
He hadn't gone a yard when –

                              Bang!

With open Jaws, a Lion sprang,
And hungrily began to eat
The Boy: beginning at his feet.

Now just imagine how it feels
When first your toes and then your heels,
And then by gradual degrees,
Your shins and ankles, calves and knees,
Are slowly eaten, bit by bit.

No wonder Jim detested it!
No wonder that he shouted 'Hi!'
The Honest Keeper heard his cry,
Though very fat

                    he almost ran
To help the little gentleman.
'Ponto!' he ordered as he came
(For Ponto was the Lion's name),
'Ponto!' he cried,

with angry Frown.
'Let go, Sir! Down, Sir! Put it down!'

The Lion made a sudden Stop,
He let the Dainty Morsel drop,
And slunk reluctant to his Cage,
Snarling with Disappointed Rage.
But when he bent him over Jim,
The Honest Keeper's

Eyes were dim.
The Lion having reached his Head,
The Miserable Boy was dead!

When Nurse informed his Parents, they
Were more Concerned than I can say: –
His Mother, as She dried her eyes,
Said, 'Well – it gives me no surprise,
He would not do as he was told!'
His Father, who was self-controlled,
Bade all the children round attend
To James' miserable end,
And always keep a-hold of Nurse
For fear of finding something worse.

Henry King

WHO CHEWED BITS OF STRING, AND WAS EARLY
CUT OFF IN DREADFUL AGONIES

The Chief Defect of Henry King
Was

chewing little bits of String.
At last he swallowed some which tied

Itself in ugly Knots inside.

Physicians of the Utmost Fame
Were called at once; but when they came
They answered,

as they took their Fees,
'There is no Cure for this Disease.
Henry will very soon be dead.'
His Parents stood about his Bed
Lamenting his Untimely Death,
When Henry, with his Latest Breath,
Cried –

'Oh, my Friends, be warned by me,

That Breakfast, Dinner, Lunch and Tea
Are all the Human Frame requires . . . '
With that the Wretched Child expires.

Matilda

WHO TOLD LIES, AND WAS BURNED TO DEATH

Matilda told such Dreadful Lies,

It made one Gasp and Stretch one's Eyes;
Her Aunt, who, from her Earliest Youth,
Had kept a Strict Regard for Truth,

———

Attempted to Believe Matilda:
The effort very nearly killed her,
And would have done so, had not She
Discovered this Infirmity.
For once, towards the Close of Day,
Matilda, growing tired of play,

And finding she was left alone,
Went tiptoe

to

the Telephone
And summoned the Immediate Aid
Of London's Noble Fire-Brigade.
Within an hour the Gallant Band
Were pouring in on every hand,
From Putney, Hackney Downs and Bow,
With Courage high and Hearts a-glow
They galloped, roaring through the Town,

'Matilda's House is Burning Down!'
Inspired by British Cheers and Loud
Proceeding from the Frenzied Crowd,
They ran their ladders through a score
Of windows on the Ball Room Floor;
And took Peculiar Pains to Souse
The Pictures up and down the House,

Until Matilda's Aunt succeeded
In showing them they were not needed
And even then she had to pay
To get the Men to go away!

·　·　·　·　·　·

It happened that a few Weeks later
Her Aunt was off to the Theatre
To see that Interesting Play

The Second Mrs Tanqueray.

She had refused to take her Niece
To hear this Entertaining Piece:
A Deprivation Just and Wise
To Punish her for Telling Lies.
That Night a Fire *did* break out –
You should have heard Matilda Shout!
You should have heard her Scream and Bawl,

And throw the window up and call
To People passing in the Street –
(The rapidly increasing Heat
Encouraging her to obtain
Their confidence) – but all in vain!
For every time She shouted 'Fire!'

They only answered 'Little Liar!'
And therefore when her Aunt returned,

Matilda, and the House, were Burned.

Godolphin Horne

WHO WAS CURSED WITH THE SIN OF PRIDE, AND BECAME A BOOT-BLACK

Godolphin Horne was Nobly Born;
He held the Human Race in Scorn,
And lived with all his Sisters where
His father lived, in Berkeley Square.
And oh! the Lad was Deathly Proud!

He never shook your Hand or Bowed,
But merely smirked and nodded

                                    thus:
How perfectly ridiculous!
Alas! That such Affected Tricks
Should flourish in a Child of Six!
(For such was Young Godolphin's age.)

Just then, the Court required a Page,
Whereat

the Lord High Chamberlain
(The Kindest and the Best of Men),
He went good-naturedly and

took
A Perfectly Enormous Book
Called *People Qualified to Be*
Attendant on His Majesty,
And murmured, as he scanned the list
(To see that no one should be missed),
'There's

William Coutts has
got the Flu,

And Billy Higgs would never do,

And Guy de Vere is far too
young,
And . . . wasn't D'Alton's Father
hung?
And as for Alexander Byng! – . . .
I think I know the kind of thing,

A Churchman, cleanly, nobly born,
Come, let us say Godolphin Horne?'
But hardly had he said the word
When Murmurs of Dissent were heard.
The King of Iceland's Eldest Son
Said, 'Thank you! I am taking none!'
The Aged Duchess of Athlone
Remarked, in her sub-acid tone,
'I doubt if He is what we need!'
With which the Bishops all agreed;
And even Lady Mary Flood
(*So* Kind, and oh! so *really* good)
Said, 'No! He wouldn't do at all,
He'd make us feel a lot too small.'
The Chamberlain said,

'. . . Well, well, well!
No doubt you're right. . . . One cannot tell!'
He took his Gold and Diamond Pen
And

Scratched Godolphin out again.
So now Godolphin is the Boy

Who blacks the Boots at the Savoy.

Rebecca

A Trick that everyone abhors
In Little Girls is slamming Doors.
A

Wealthy Banker's

42

Little Daughter

Who lived in Palace Green, Bayswater
(By name Rebecca Offendort),
Was given to this Furious Sport.

She would
  deliberately go

And Slam the
  door like
    Billy-Ho!

To make

her

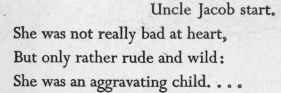

Uncle Jacob start.
She was not really bad at heart,
But only rather rude and wild:
She was an aggravating child. . . .

It happened that a Marble Bust
Of Abraham was standing just
Above the Door this little Lamb
Had carefully prepared to Slam,
And Down it came! It knocked her flat!

It laid her out! She looked
like that.

Her funeral Sermon (which was long
And followed by a Sacred Song)
Mentioned her Virtues, it is true,
But dwelt upon her Vices too,

And showed the Dreadful End of One
Who goes and slams the door for Fun.

The children who were brought to hear
The awful Tale from far and near
Were much impressed,

and inly swore
They never more would slam the Door.
– As often they had done before.

Charles Augustus Fortescue

WHO ALWAYS DID WHAT WAS RIGHT, AND SO
ACCUMULATED AN IMMENSE FORTUNE

The nicest child I ever knew
Was Charles Augustus Fortescue.
He never lost his cap, or tore
His stockings or his pinafore:
In eating Bread he made no Crumbs,
He was extremely fond of sums,
To which, however,
   he preferred
The Parsing of a
   Latin Word –
He sought, when it
   was in his power,
For information
   twice an hour,

And as for finding Mutton-Fat
Unappetising, far from that!
He often, at his Father's Board,
Would beg them, of his own accord,

To give him, if they did not mind,
The Greasiest Morsels they could find –
His Later Years did not belie
The Promise of his Infancy.

In Public Life he always tried
To take a judgement Broad and Wide;

In Private, none was more than he
Renowned for quiet courtesy.
He rose at once in his Career,
And long before his Fortieth Year
Had wedded

Fifi,

Only Child
Of Bunyan, First Lord Aberfylde.
He thus became immensely Rich,
And built the Splendid Mansion which
Is called

"The Cedars, Muswell Hill,"

Where he resides in Affluence still
To show what Everybody might
Become by
SIMPLY DOING RIGHT.

New
Cautionary Tales

ILLUSTRATED BY
NICOLAS BENTLEY

Sarah Byng

WHO COULD NOT READ AND WAS TOSSED

INTO A THORNY HEDGE BY A BULL

Some years ago you heard me sing
My doubts on Alexander Byng.
His sister Sarah now inspires
My jaded Muse, my failing fires.
Of Sarah Byng the tale is told
How when the child was twelve years old
She could not read or write a line.

———

Her sister Jane, though barely nine,
Could spout the Catechism through

And parts of Matthew Arnold too,

While little Bill
  who came between

Was quite unnaturally keen
  On
    'Athalie', by Jean Racine.

But not so Sarah! Not so Sal!
She was a most uncultured girl

Who didn't care a pinch of snuff
For any literary stuff

And gave the classics all a miss.
Observe the consequence of this!
As she was walking home one day,
Upon the fields across her way
A gate, securely padlocked, stood,
And by its side a piece of wood
On which was painted plain and full,

BEWARE THE VERY
FURIOUS BULL.

Alas!
  The young illiter-
    ate
Went blindly for-
    ward to her fate,
And ignorantly
    climbed the gate!

Now happily the Bull that day
Was rather in the mood for play
Than goring people through and through
As Bulls so very often do;

He tossed her lightly with his horns
Into a prickly hedge of thorns,
And stood by laughing while she strode
And pushed and struggled to the road.

The lesson was not lost upon
The child, who since has always gone
A long way round to keep away
From signs, whatever they may say,
And leaves a padlocked gate alone.
Moreoever she has wisely grown
Confirmed in her instinctive guess

That literature breeds distress.

Jack and his Pony, Tom

Jack had a little pony – Tom;
He frequently would take it from

The stable where it used to stand
And give it sugar with his hand.

He also gave it oats and hay
And carrots twenty times a day
And grass in basketfuls, and greens,
And swedes and mangolds, also beans,
And patent foods from various sources
And bread (which isn't good for horses)
And chocolate and apple-rings
And lots and lots of other things
The most of which do not agree
With Polo Ponies such as he.
And all in such a quantity
As ruined his digestion wholly
And turned him from a Ponopoly
– I mean a Polo Pony – into
A case that clearly must be seen to.

Because he swelled and swelled and swelled.
Which, when the kindly boy beheld,

He gave him medicine by the pail
And malted milk, and nutmeg ale,
And yet it only swelled the more
Until its stomach touched the floor,

And then it heaved and groaned as well
And staggered, till at last it fell
And found it could not rise again.
Jack wept and prayed – but all in vain.

The pony died, and as it died
Kicked him severely in the side.

MORAL

Kindness to animals should be
Attuned to their brutality.

Tom and his Pony, Jack

Tom had a little pony, Jack:

He vaulted lightly on its back
And galloped off for miles and miles,
A-leaping hedges, gates and stiles,

And shouting 'Yoicks!' and 'Tally-Ho!'
And 'Heads I win!' and 'Tails below!'

And many another sporting phrase.
He rode like this for several days,
Until the pony, feeling tired,
Collapsed, looked heavenward and expired.

His father made a fearful row.
He said 'By Gum, you've done it now!
Here lies – a carcase on the ground –
No less than five and twenty pound!

Indeed the value of the beast
Would probably have much increased.
His teeth were false; and all were told

That he was only four
    years old.
Oh! Curse it all! I tell you plain
I'll never let you ride again.'

MORAL

His father died when he was twenty
And left three horses, which is plenty.

About John

WHO LOST A FORTUNE BY THROWING STONES

JOHN VAVASSOUR
DE QUENTIN JONES

Was very fond
of throwing
stones

At Horses, People,
Passing Trains,
But specially at
Window-panes.

Like many of the
Upper Class
He liked the
Sound of
Broken
Glass[1]

1. A line I stole with subtle daring
From Wing-Commander Maurice Baring

It bucked him up and made him gay:
It was his favourite form of Play.
But the Amusement cost him dear,
My children, as you now shall hear.

JOHN VAVASSOUR DE QUENTIN had
An uncle, who adored the lad:

And often chuckled, 'Wait until
You see what's left you in my will!'

Nor were the words without import,
Because this uncle did a sort
Of something in the City, which
Had made him fabulously rich.
(Although his brother, John's papa,
Was poor, as many fathers are.)

He had a lot of stocks and shares
And half a street in Buenos Aires, [1]
A bank in Rio, and a line
Of Steamers to the Argentine.
And options more than I can tell,
And bits of Canada as well;
He even had a mortgage on
The House inhabited by John.
His will, the cause of all the fuss,
Was carefully indited thus:

[1]. But this pronunciation varies.
     Some people call it Bu-enos Airés.

'This is the last and solemn Will
Of Uncle William – known as Bill.

I do bequeath, devise and give
By Execution Mandative
The whole amount of what I've got
(It comes to a tremendous lot!)
In seizin to devolve upon
My well-beloved nephew John.

(And here the witnesses will sign
Their names upon the dotted line.)'

Such was the Legal Instrument
Expressing Uncle Bill's intent.

As time went on declining Health
Transmogrified this Man of Wealth;
And it was excellently clear
That Uncle Bill's demise was near.

At last his sole idea of fun
Was sitting snoozling in
the sun.

So once, when he
would take the air,
They wheeled him in
his Patent Chair

(By 'They', I mean his Nurse, who came
From Dorchester upon the Thame:
Miss Charming was the Nurse's name),
To where beside a little wood
A long abandoned green-house stood,
And there he sank into a doze
Of senile and inept repose.
But not for long his drowsy ease!
A stone came whizzing through the trees,
And caught him smartly in the eye.
He woke with an appalling cry,
And shrieked in agonizing tones:
'Oh! Lord! Whoever's throwing stones!'

Miss Charming, who was standing near,
Said: 'That was Master John, I fear!'

'Go, get my Ink-pot and my Quill,
My Blotter and my Famous Will.'

Miss Charming flew as though on wings
To fetch these necessary things,
And Uncle William ran his pen
Through 'well-beloved John', and then
Proceeded, in the place of same,
To substitute Miss Charming's name:

Who now resides in Portman Square
And is accepted everywhere.

Peter Goole

WHO RUINED HIS FATHER AND MOTHER BY EXTRAVAGANCE

PART I

Young Peter Goole, a child of
  nine
Gave little reason to complain.
Though an imaginative youth
He very often told the truth,
And never tried to black the
  eyes
Of Comrades of superior size.

He did his lessons (more or less)
Without extravagant distress,
And showed sufficient intellect,
But failed in one severe defect;
It seems he wholly lacked a sense
Of limiting the day's expense,
And money ran between his hands
Like water through the Ocean Sands.
Such conduct could not but affect
His parent's fortune, which was wrecked
Like many and many another one
By folly in a spendthrift son:
By that most tragical mischance,
An Only Child's Extravagance.

There came a day when Mr Goole
– The Father of this little fool –
With nothing in the bank at all
Was up against it, like a wall.

He wrang his hands, exclaiming, 'If

I only had a bit of Stiff
How different would be my life!'
Whereat his true and noble wife

Replied, to comfort him, 'Alas!
I said that this would come to pass!
Nothing can keep us off the rocks
But Peter's little Money Box.'
The Father, therefore (and his wife),

They prised it open with a knife —

But nothing could be found therein
Save two bone buttons and a pin.

PART II

They had to sell the house and grounds

For less than twenty thousand pounds,

And so retired,

with broken hearts,

To vegetate in foreign parts,

And ended their declining years
At Blidah – which is near Algiers.
There in the course of time
         they died,

And there lie buried
     side by side.

While when we turn to Peter, he
The cause of this catastrophe,
There fell upon him such a fate
As makes me shudder to relate.
Just in its fifth and final year,
His University Career
Was blasted by the new and dread
Necessity of earning bread.
He was compelled to join a firm
Of Brokers – in the summer term!

And even now, at twenty-five,

He has to
WORK
    to
keep alive!

Yes! All day long from 10 till 4!
For half the year or even more;

With but an hour or two to spend
At luncheon with a city friend.

The Bad Child's Book
of Beasts

ILLUSTRATED BY
B. T. B.

Introduction

I call you bad, my little child,
  Upon the title page,
Because a manner rude and wild
  Is common at your age.

The Moral of this priceless work
  (If rightly understood)
Will make you – from a little Turk –
  Unnaturally good.

Do not as evil children do,
  Who on the slightest grounds
Will imitate

the Kangaroo,
With wild unmeaning bounds:

Do not as children badly bred,
   Who eat like little Hogs,
And when they have to go to bed
   Will Whine like Puppy Dogs:

Who take their manners from the Ape,
   Their habits from the Bear,
Indulge the loud unseemly jape,
   And never brush their hair.

But so control your actions that
Your friends may all repeat:

'This child is dainty as the Cat,
And as the Owl discreet.'

The Polar Bear

The Polar Bear is unaware

Of cold that cuts me through:
For why? He has a coat of hair.
I wish I had one too!

———

The Lion

The Lion, the Lion, he dwells in the waste,
He has a big head and a very small waist;

But his shoulders are stark, and his jaws they
    are grim,
And a good little child will not play with him.

———

The Tiger

The Tiger on the other hand,

                        is kittenish and mild,
He makes a pretty playfellow for any little
    child;
And mothers of large families (who claim to
    common sense)

Will find a Tiger well repays the trouble and
    expense.

The Whale

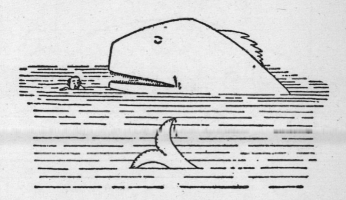

The Whale that wanders round the Pole

Is not

a table fish.
You cannot bake or boil him whole
Nor serve him in a dish;

But you may cut his blubber up
And melt it down for oil.

And so replace

the colza bean
(A product of the soil).

These facts should all be noted down
   And ruminated on,

By every Boy in Oxford town
   Who wants to be a Don.

The Hippopotamus

I shoot the Hippopotamus

with bullets made of platinum,

Because if I use leaden ones

his hide is sure to flatten 'em.

The Elephant

When people call this beast to mind,

They marvel more and more

At such a

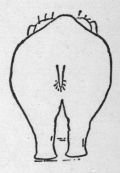

LITTLE tail behind,

So *LARGE* a trunk before.

The Rhinoceros

Rhinoceros, your hide looks all undone,

You do not take my fancy in the least:

You have a horn where other brutes have none:
Rhinoceros, you are an ugly beast.

The Frog

Be kind and tender to the Frog,

And do not call him names,
As 'Slimy skin', or 'Polly-wog',
   Or likewise 'Ugly James',
Or 'Gap-a-grin', or 'Toad-gone-wrong',
   Or 'Billy Bandy-knees':

The Frog is justly sensitive
   To epithets like these.

No animal will more repay
   A treatment kind and fair;
At least

        so lonely people say
Who keep a frog (and, by the way,
They are extremely rare).

More Beasts
for Worse Children

ILLUSTRATED BY
B. T. B.

Oh! My!

Introduction

The parents of the learned child
  (His father and his mother)
Were utterly aghast to note
The facts he would at random quote

On creatures curious, rare and wild;
  And wondering, asked each other:

'An idle little child like this,
  How is it that he knows

—

What years of close analysis
    Are powerless to disclose?
Our brains are trained, our books are big,
    And yet we always fail

To answer why the Guinea-pig
    Is born without a tail.

Or why the Wanderoo should rant[1]
    In wild, unmeaning rhymes,

1. Sometimes called the 'Lion-tailed or tufted Baboon of Ceylon'.

Whereas the Indian Elephant
Will only read *The Times*.

Perhaps he found a way to slip
Unnoticed to the Zoo,

And gave the Pachyderm a tip,
   Or pumped the Wanderoo.

Or even by an artful plan
   Deceived our watchful eyes,
And interviewed the Pelican,
Who is extremely wise.'

'Oh! no,' said he, in humble tone,
   With shy but conscious look,

'Such facts I never could have known
But for this little book.'

The Python

A Python I should not advise, –
It needs a doctor for its eyes,
And has the measles yearly.

However, if you feel inclined
To get one (to improve your mind,
And not from fashion merely),
Allow no music near its cage;

And when it flies into a rage
Chastise it, most severely.

I had an aunt in Yucatan
Who bought a Python from a man
    And kept it for a pet.
She died, because she never knew
These simple little rules and few; –

The Snake is living yet.

The Porcupine

What! would you slap the Porcupine?
    Unhappy child – desist!
Alas! that any friend of mine
    Should turn Tupto-philist.[1]

---

1. From τύπτω = I strike; φιλέω = I love; one that loves to strike.
The word is not found in classical Greek, nor does it occur among
the writers of the Renaissance – nor anywhere else.

To strike the meanest and the least
Of creatures is a sin,

How much more bad to beat a beast
With prickles on its skin.

The Llama

The Llama is a woolly sort of fleecy hairy
  goat,
With an indolent expression and an undulating
  throat
  Like an unsuccessful literary man.

———

And I know the place he lives in (or at least –
    I think I do)
It is Ecuador, Brazil or Chile – possibly Peru;
    You must find it in the Atlas if you can.

The Llama of the Pampasses you never should
confound
(In spite of a deceptive similarity of sound)
With the Lama who is Lord of Turkestan.

For the former is a beautiful and valuable
    beast,

But the latter is not lovable nor useful in the
    least;

And the Ruminant is preferable surely to the
    Priest

Who battens on the woeful superstitions of the
    East,

    The Mongol of the Monastery of Shan.

The Microbe

The Microbe is so very small
You cannot make him out at all,
But many sanguine people hope
To see him through a microscope.
His jointed tongue that lies beneath
A hundred curious rows of teeth;
His seven tufted tails with lots
Of lovely pink and purple spots,

On each of which a pattern
        stands,
Composed of forty separate
        bands;
His eyebrows of a tender
        green;
All these have never yet been seen –
But Scientists, who ought to know,
Assure us that they must be so. . . .
Oh! Let us never, never doubt
What nobody is sure about!

MORE PEERS

Verses by H. BELLOC
Pictures by B. T. B.

Lord Roehampton

During a late election Lord
Roehampton strained a vocal chord
From shouting, very loud and high,
To lots and lots of people why
The Budget in his own opin-
-Ion should not be allowed to win.

He

        sought a Specialist, who said:
'You have a swelling in the head:
Your Larynx is a thought relaxed
And you are greatly over-taxed.'
'I am indeed! On every side!'
The Earl (for such he was) replied.

In hoarse excitement. . . . 'Oh! My Lord,
You jeopardize your vocal chord!'
Broke in the worthy Specialist.
'Come! Here's the treatment! I insist!
To Bed! to Bed! And do not speak
A single word till Wednesday week,
When I will come and set you free
(If you are cured) and take my fee.'
On Wednesday week the Doctor hires
A Brand-new Car with Brand-new Tyres

And Brand-new Chauffeur all complete
For visiting South Audley Street.

. . .

But what is this? No Union Jack
Floats on the Stables at the back!
No Toffs escorting Ladies fair
Perambulate the Gay Parterre.
A 'Scutcheon hanging lozenge-wise
And draped in crape appals his eyes
Upon the mansion's ample door,
To which he wades through

heaps of Straw,

1. This is the first and only time
   That I have used this sort of Rhyme.

And which a Butler, drowned in tears,
On opening but confirms his fears:
'Oh! Sir! – Prepare to hear the worst!...
Last night my kind old master burst.
And what is more, I doubt if he
Has left enough to pay your fee.
The Budget –'

With a dreadful oath,
The Specialist,

denouncing both
The Budget *and* the House of Lords,
Buzzed angrily Bayswaterwards.

And ever since, as I am told,
Gets it beforehand; and in gold.

Lord Epsom

A Horse, Lord Epsom did bestride
With mastery and quiet pride.
He dug his spurs into its hide.

The Horse,

discerning it was pricked,

Incontinently

bucked and kicked,
A thing that no one could predict!

Lord Epsom clearly understood
The High-bred creature's nervous mood,

As only such a horseman could.

Dismounting,

he was heard to say
That it was kinder to delay
His pleasure to a future day.

*

He had the Hunter led away.

Lord Hippo

Lord Hippo suffered fearful loss

By putting money on a horse
Which he believed, if it were pressed,
Would run far faster than the rest:
For

someone who was in the know

Had confidently told him so.

But

on the morning of the race

It only took

the *seventh* place!

Picture the Viscount's great surprise!
He scarcely could believe his eyes!
He sought the Individual who
Had laid him odds at 9 to 2,

Suggesting as a useful tip
That they should enter Partnership
And put to joint account the debt
Arising from his foolish bet.

But when the Bookie – oh! my word,
I only wish you could have heard
The way he roared he did not think,
And hoped that they might strike him pink!
Lord Hippo simply turned and ran
From this infuriated man.

Despairing, maddened and distraught
He utterly collapsed and sought
His sire,

     the Earl of Potamus,
And brokenly addressed him thus:
'Dread Sire – to-day – at Ascot – I . . . '
His genial parent made reply:

'Come! Come! Come! Come! Don't look so
   glum!
Trust your Papa and name the sum. . . .

WHAT?

. . . *Fifteen hundred thousand?* . . . Hum!
However . . . stiffen up, you wreck;
Boys will be boys – so here's the cheque!'

Lord Hippo, feeling deeply – well,
More grateful than he cared to tell –
Punted the lot on Little Nell : –
And got a telegram at dinner

To say

that he had backed the Winner !

Lord Lucky

Lord Lucky, by a curious fluke,
Became a most important duke.
From living in a vile Hotel

A long way east of Camberwell

He rose in less than half an hour
To riches, dignity and power.
It happened in the following way: —
The Real Duke went out one day
To shoot with several people, one

Of whom had never used a gun.
This gentleman (a Mr Meyer
Of Rabley Abbey, Rutlandshire),
As he was scrambling through the brake,

Discharged his weapon by mistake,
And plugged about an ounce of lead
Piff-bang into his Grace's Head –
Who naturally fell down dead.

His heir, Lord Ugly, roared, 'You Brute!

Take that to teach you how to shoot!'
Whereat he volleyed left and right;
But being somewhat short of sight,
His right-hand Barrel only got
The second heir, Lord Poddleplot;
The while the left-hand charge (or choke)
Accounted for another bloke,
Who stood with an astounded air

Bewildered by the whole affair
– And was the third remaining heir.
After the

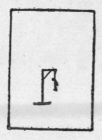

Execution (which
Is something rare among the Rich)
Lord Lucky, while of course, he needed

Some

    help to prove his claim,

                    succeeded.

– But after his succession, though
All this was over years ago,
He only once indulged the whim
Of asking Meyer to lunch with him.

Lord Abbott

Lord Abbott's coronet was far too small,
So small, that as he sauntered down Whitehall
Even the youthful Proletariat
(Who probably mistook it for a Hat)
Remarked on its exiguous extent.

Here is a picture of the incident.

Ladies
and Gentlemen

ILLUSTRATED BY
NICOLAS BENTLEY

The Garden Party

The Rich arrived in pairs
And also in Rólls Royces;

They talked of their affairs
In loud and strident voices.

(The Husbands and the Wives
Of this select society
Lead independent lives
Of infinite variety.)

The Poor arrived in Fords,
Whose features they resembled,

They laughed to see so many Lords
And Ladies all assembled.

The People in Between
Looked underdone and harassed,

And out of place and mean,
And horribly embarrassed.

For the hoary social curse
Gets hoarier and hoarier,
And it stinks a trifle worse
Than in
The days of Queen Victoria,

when

They married and gave in marriage,
They danced at the County Ball,
And some of them kept a carriage.

AND THE FLOOD DESTROYED THEM ALL

The Three Races

I

Behold, my child,
    the Nordic Man
And be as like
    him as you can.
His legs are long;
    his mind is slow;
His hair is lank
    and made of tow.

II

And here we have the Alpine Race.
Oh! What a broad and foolish face!

His skin is of a dirty yellow,
He is a most unpleasant fellow.

III

The most degraded of them all
Mediterranean we call.
His hair is crisp, and even curls,

And he is saucy with the girls.

Obiter Dicta

I

SIR HENRY WAFFLE K.C. (*continuing*)

Sir Anthony Habberton, Justice and Knight,
Was enfeoffed of two acres of land

And it doesn't
    sound much
        till you hear that the site
    Was a strip to the South of the Strand.

HIS LORDSHIP (*Obiter Dictum*)

    A strip of the South of the Strand
    Is a good situation for land.

———

It is healthy and dry
And sufficiently high
And convenient on every hand.

II

SIR HENRY WAFFLE K.C. (*continuing*)

Now Sir Anthony, shooting in Timberley Wood,
Was imprudent enough to take cold;
And he

died without warning at six in the morning,
Because he was awfully old.

HIS LORDSHIP (*Obiter Dictum*)

I have often been credibly told
That when people are awfully old
Though cigars are a curse

And

strong waters are worse

There is nothing so fatal as cold.

III

SIR HENRY WAFFLE K.C. (*continuing*)

But Archibald answered on hearing the news : —
'I never move out till I must.'
Which was all very jolly for *Cestui que Use*
But the Devil for *Cestui que Trust.*

HIS LORDSHIP (*Obiter Dictum*)
The office of *Cestui que Trust*
Is reserved for the learned and just.
Any villain you choose
May be *Cestui que Use*,
But a Lawyer for *Cestui que Trust.*

IV

SIR HENRY WAFFLE K.C. (*continuing*)

Now the ruling laid down
in *Regina v. Brown*
May be cited. . . .

HIS LORDSHIP (*rising energetically*)

You're wrong!
It may not!

I've strained all
my powers
For some thirty-six hours
To unravel this pestilent rot.

THE WHOLE COURT (*rising and singing in chorus*)

Your Lordship is sound to the core.

It is nearly a quarter to four.

We've had quite enough

       Of this horrible stuff

And we don't want to hear any more!

LITTLE SILLY MAN (*rising at the back of the Court*)
Your Lordship is perfectly right.

He can't go on rhyming all night.
I suggest. . . .
(*He is gagged, bound and dragged off to a Dungeon.*)

The Example

John Henderson, an unbeliever,
Had lately lost his Joie de Vivre
From reading far too many books.
He went about with gloomy looks;
Despair inhabited his breast
And made the man a perfect pest.
Not so his sister, Mary Lunn,
She had a whacking lot of fun!
Though unbelieving as a beast
She didn't worry in the least.

But drank as hard as she was able

And sang and danced upon the table;

And

when she met her brother Jack

She used to smack him on the back
So smartly as to make him jump,
And cry, 'What-ho! You've got the hump!'
A phrase which, more than any other,
Was gall and wormwood to her brother;
For, having an agnostic mind,
He was exceedingly refined.

The Christians, a declining band,
Would point with monitory hand

To Henderson his desperation,
To Mary Lunn her dissipation,
And often mutter, 'Mark my words!
Something will happen to those birds!'

Which came to pass: for

Mary Lunn
Died suddenly, at ninety-one,

Of Psittacosis, not before
Becoming an appalling bore.
While Henderson, I'm glad to state,
Though naturally celibate,
Married an intellectual wife
Who made him lead the Higher life

And

    wouldn't give him any wine;
Whereby he fell in a decline,
And, at the time of writing this,
Is suffering from paralysis,
The which, we hear with no surprise,
Will shortly end in his demise.

MORAL

The moral is (it is indeed!)
You mustn't monkey with the Creed.

THE CALL OF THE WILD
Jack London

This tale of a dog's fight for survival in the harsh and frozen Yukon is one of the greatest animal stories ever written. It tells of a dog born to luxury but sold as a sledge dog, and how he rises magnificently above all his enemies to become one of the most feared and admired dogs in the north.

LITTLE WOMEN
L. M. Alcott

The good-natured March girls – Meg, Jo, Beth and Amy – manage to lead interesting lives despite their father's absence at war and the family's lack of money. Whether they're making plans for putting on a play or forming a secret society, their enthusiasm is infectious. Even Laurie, the rich but lonely boy next door, is swept up in their gaiety. (*Good Wives*, *Little Men* and *Jo's Boys* are also published in Puffin Classics)

MOONFLEET
J. Meade Falkner

Most of the inhabitants of the tiny village of Moonfleet are either smugglers or fishermen, so it's no surprise when 15-year-old John Trenchard gets involved in the smuggling business. Eventually he is forced to leave the country with a price on his head, and only returns to England after a long and difficult period abroad.

THE WIZARD OF OZ
L. Frank Baum

Surely the best loved of all modern fairy tales: a magical story in which Dorothy, together with her companions the Tin Woodman, the Scarecrow and the Cowardly Lion, makes her enchanting journey along the yellow brick road in search of the wonderful Wizard – a journey that takes her to the City of Emeralds.

THE ADVENTURES OF TOM SAWYER
Mark Twain

The famous tale of a boy's life in a small town on the banks of the Mississippi River, Tom skips school and with his friends, Huck Finn and Jim, spends his days on mad adventures – some real, some imagined. Like Tom himself, this book is happy and cheerful, exciting but also funny.

THE CHILDREN OF THE NEW FOREST
Captain Marryat

England in 1647: the country is divided as Cavaliers and Roundheads fight bitterly to decide who should rule. The four Beverley children lose their parents in the war and are forced to go into hiding. Ill-prepared for a life on the land, and always at great risk of discovery, they set about hunting and housekeeping with great spirit and courage.

WHAT KATY DID
Susan Coolidge

The moving story of how Katy Carr overcame her tragic accident and learned to be as loving and as patient as the beautiful invalid, Helen.

KIDNAPPED
R. L. Stevenson

A swashbuckling tale of kidnap and murder, set in the Scottish Highlands after the Jacobite Rebellion. It tells of the flight of young David Balfour after he is treacherously cheated of his rightful estate and then wrongly suspected of murder.

THE LOST WORLD
Sir Arthur Conan Doyle

Journalist Ed Malone is looking for an adventure, and that's exactly what he finds when he meets the eccentric Professor Challenger: an adventure that leads Malone and his three companions deep into the Amazon jungle, to a lost world where dinosaurs roam free and the natives fight out a murderous war with their fierce neighbours, the ape-men.

HORNBLOWER GOES TO SEA
C. S. Forester

The dramatic sea-battles and adventures Hornblower faces take him from being a quiet yet strangely impressive young man, newly commissioned into Nelson's navy, to an intrepid commander on the high seas, making his mark as one of the most formidable officers ever to set sail.

THE HOUSE OF ARDEN
E. Nesbit

There's no end to the Arden magic, as Edred and Elfrida soon find out – with a little help from the Mouldiwarp, a rather bad-tempered white mole. But it's pretty hard work unexpectedly inheriting a title, moving into a castle which needs to be explored *and* travelling back in time in search of hidden treasure!

THE PRINCE AND THE PAUPER
Mark Twain

Tom Canty and Edward Tudor, pauper and prince, exchange identities and see just how the other half lives. This is a richly entertaining tale of wild escapades and madcap scrapes, but with a layer of serious social criticism.

DR JEKYLL AND MR HYDE
Robert Louis Stevenson

Dr Jekyll is a respectable gentleman, admired and well-liked. But when his secret scientific experiments go horribly awry, he is plunged into a furtive, tortuous existence, a living nightmare from which it becomes increasingly difficult to escape . . .

THE HOUND OF THE BASKERVILLES
Sir Arthur Conan Doyle

When Sir Charles Baskerville dies mysteriously in the grounds of Baskerville Hall, Sherlock Holmes is called in to investigate. Everyone remembers the terrible legend of a diabolical creature that haunts the moor. Will the greatest detective in the world be defeated by a hound from hell?

GRIMMS' FAIRY TALES

From the land of castles, lakes and dark forests, the Brothers Grimm brought a host of enchanting fairy tales, inhabited by giants and dwarfs, princesses and witches, birds and beasts. The fascinating folk-tales hold a timeless magic which has enthralled children since the beginning of the nineteenth century.